Norman Batte

Draw
Seascapes

Series editors: David and Brenda Herbert

A & C Black · London

First published 1980
New style of paperback binding 1997
by A & C Black (Publishers) Limited
35 Bedford Row, London WC1R 4JH

Reprinted 1999

ISBN 0-7136-4857-0

Printed in Great Britain by Martins the Printers, Berwick-upon-Tweed

Contents

Making a start

This book is for those who have done little, if any, drawing before, as well as for more experienced artists who want to specialise in seascapes. Remember that there are many different kinds of seascape—from crowded beach scenes to lonely rocky coves, from ships in storms to quiet, busy harbours; and that there are many different objects on seashores, so that there is no lack of variety in what you can draw. These pages show only a few of the subjects possible to you, but I hope they will be encouraging. Drawing seascapes is a fascinating pastime, open to anyone; full of fun—and fresh air.

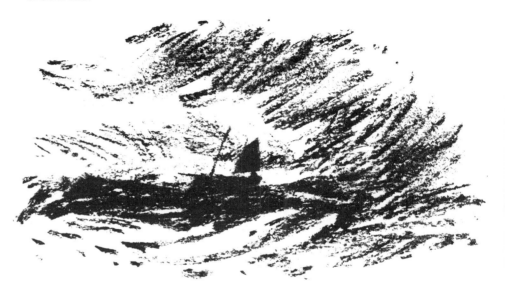

Learning to draw is largely a matter of practice and observation—so draw as much and as often as you can, and use your eyes all the time.

The time you spend on a drawing is not important. A ten-minute sketch can say more than a slow, painstaking drawing that takes many hours.

Carry a sketchbook with you whenever possible, and don't be shy of using it in public, either for quick notes to be used later or for a finished drawing.

To do an interesting drawing, you must enjoy it. Even if you start on something that doesn't particularly interest you, you will probably find that the act of drawing it—and looking at it in a new way—creates its own excitement. The less you think about how you are drawing and the more you think about what you are drawing, the better your drawing will be.

The best equipment will not itself make you a better artist—a masterpiece can be drawn with a stump of pencil on a scrap of paper. But good equipment is encouraging and pleasant to use, so buy the best you can afford and don't be afraid to use it freely.

Be as bold as you dare. It's your piece of paper and you can do what you like with it. Experiment with the biggest piece of paper and the boldest, softest piece of chalk or crayon you can find, filling the paper with lines—scribbles, funny faces, lettering, anything—to get a feeling of freedom. Even if you think you have a gift for tiny delicate line drawings with a fine pen or pencil, this is worth trying. It will act as a 'loosening up' exercise. The results may surprise you.

Be self-critical. If a drawing looks wrong, scrap it and start again. A second, third or even fourth attempt will often be better than the first, because you are learning more about the subject all the time. Use an eraser as little as possible—piecemeal correction won't help. Don't re-trace your lines. If a line is right the first time, leave it alone—heavier re-drawing leads to a dull mechanical look.

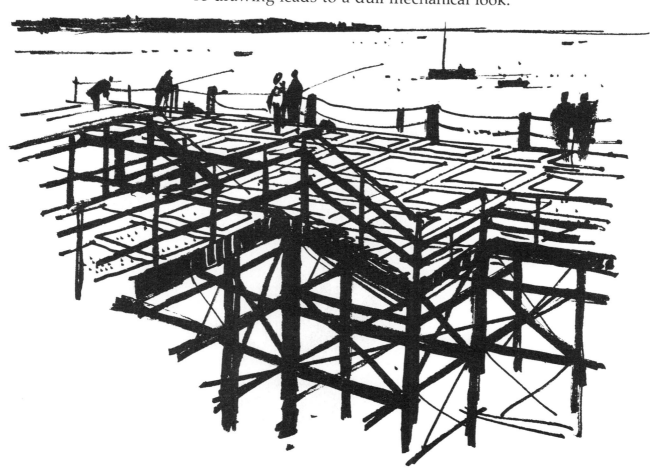

Try drawing in colour. Dark blue, reddish-brown and dark green are good drawing colours. A coloured pencil, pen or chalk can often be very useful for detail, emphasis or contrast on a black and white drawing.

You can learn a certain amount from copying other people's drawings. But you will learn more from a drawing done from direct observation of the subject or even out of your head, however stiff and unsatisfactory the results may seem at first.

A lot can be learned by practice and from books, but a teacher can be a great help. If you get the chance, don't hesitate to join a class—even one evening a week can do a lot of good.

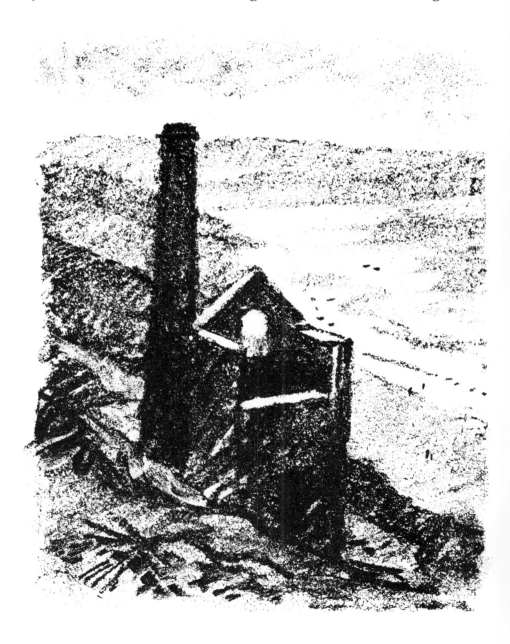

What to draw with

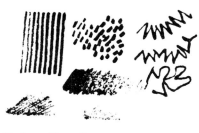

Carbon Pencil

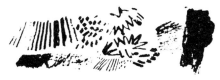

Charcoal

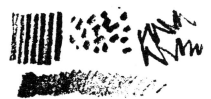

Wax crayon

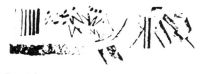

Conté

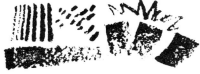

Oil pastel

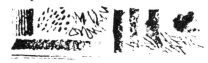

Soft chalk pastel

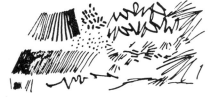

Pen and ink

Pencils are graded according to hardness, from 6H (the hardest) through 5H, 4H, 3H, 2H to H; then HB, through 1B, 2B, 3B, 4B, 5B up to 6B (the softest). For most purposes, a soft pencil (HB or softer) is best. If you keep it sharp, it will draw as fine a line as a hard pencil but with less pressure, which makes it easier to control. Sometimes it is effective to smudge the line with your finger or an eraser, but if you do this too much the drawing will look woolly.

Charcoal (which is very soft) is excellent for large, bold sketches, but not for detail. If you use it, beware of accidental smudging. A drawing can even be dusted or rubbed off the paper altogether. To prevent this, preserve your drawing with spray fixative. Charcoal pencils such as the Royal Sovereign are also very useful.

Wax crayons (also soft) are not easily smudged or erased. You can scrape a line away from a drawing on good quality paper, or partly scrape a drawing to get special effects.

Conté crayons, wood-cased or in solid sticks, are available in various degrees of hardness, and in three colours—black, red and white. The cased crayons are easy to sharpen, but the solid sticks are more fun—you can use the side of the stick for large areas of tone. Conté is harder than charcoal, but it is also easy to smudge. The black is very intense.

Pastels (available in a wide range of colours) are softer still. Since drawings in pastel are usually called 'paintings', they are really beyond the scope of this book.

Pens vary as much as pencils or crayons. The Gillot 659 is a very popular crowquill pen. Ink has a quality of its own, but of course it cannot be erased. Mapping pens are only suitable for delicate detail and minute cross-hatching.

Special artist's pens such as the Gillot 303, or the Gillot 404, allow you a more varied line, according to the angle at which you hold them and the pressure you use.

Reed, bamboo and quill pens are good for bold lines. You can make the nib end narrower or wider with the help of a sharp knife or razor blade. This kind of pen has to be dipped frequently into the ink.

Fountain pens have a softer touch than dip-in pens, and many artists prefer them.

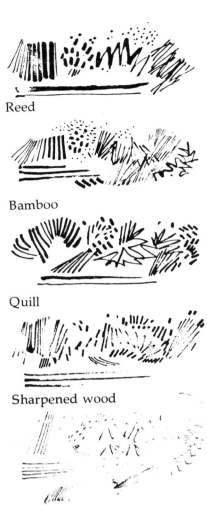

Reed

Bamboo

Quill

Sharpened wood

Ball point pen

Fibre tip pen

Brush and writing ink

Pen and brush on wet paper

Special fountain pens, such as Rapidograph and Rotring, control the flow of ink by means of a needle valve in a fine tube (the nib). Nibs are available in several grades of fineness and are interchangeable. The line they produce is of even thickness, but on coarse paper you can draw an interesting broken line similar to that of a crayon. These pens have to be held at a right-angle to the paper, which is a disadvantage.

Inks also vary. Waterproof Indian ink quickly clogs the pen. Pelikan Fount India, which is nearly as black, flows more smoothly and does not leave a varnishy deposit on the pen. Ordinary fountain-pen or writing inks (black, blue, green or brown) are less opaque, so give a drawing more variety of tone. You can mix water with any ink in order to make it even thinner. But if you are using Indian ink, add distilled or rain water, because ordinary water will cause it to curdle.

Ball point pens make a drawing look a bit mechanical, but they are cheap and fool-proof and useful for quick notes and scribbles.

Fibre pens are only slightly better, and their points tend to wear down quickly.

Felt pens are useful for quick notes and sketches, but are not good for more elaborate and finished drawings.

Brushes are most versatile drawing instruments. The Chinese and Japanese know this and until recently never used anything else, even for writing. The biggest sable brush has a fine point, and the smallest brush laid on its side provides a line broader than the broadest nib. You can add depth and variety to a pen or crayon drawing by washing over it with a brush dipped in clean water.

Mixed methods are often pleasing. Try making drawings with pen and pencil, pen and wash or Conté and wash. And try drawing with a pen on wet paper. Pencil and Conté does not look well together, and Conté will not draw over pencil or any greasy surface.

What to draw on

Try as many different surfaces as possible.

Ordinary, inexpensive paper is often as good as anything else: for example, brown and buff wrapping paper (Kraft paper) and lining for wallpaper have surfaces which are particularly suitable for charcoal and soft crayons. Some writing and duplicating papers are best for pen drawings. But there are many papers and brands made specially for the artist.

Bristol board is a smooth, hard white board designed for fine pen work.

Ledger Bond paper ("cartridge" in the UK) the most usual drawing paper, is available in a variety of surfaces—smooth, 'not surface' (semi-rough), rough.

Watercolour papers also come in various grades of smoothness. They are thick, high-quality papers, expensive but pleasant to use.

Ingres paper is mainly for pastel drawings. It has a soft, furry surface and is made in many light colours—grey, pink, blue, buff, etc.

Sketchbooks, made up from nearly all these papers, are available. Choose one with thin, smooth paper to begin with. Thin paper means more pages, and a smooth surface is best to record detail.

Lay-out pads make useful sketchbooks. Although their covers are not stiff, you can easily insert a stiff piece of card to act as firm backing to your drawing. The paper is semi-transparent, but this can be useful—almost as tracing paper—if you want to make a new, improved version of your last drawing.

An improvised sketchbook can be just as good as a bought one—or better. Find two pieces of thick card, sandwich a stack of paper, preferably of different kinds, between them and clip together.

Examples showing the use of different surfaces and different drawing instruments appear on the next two pages.

Carbon pencil on flimsy detail paper

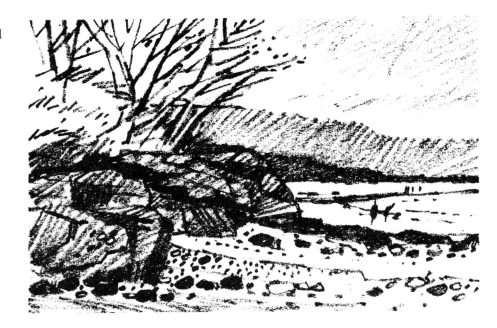

Pencil on writing paper

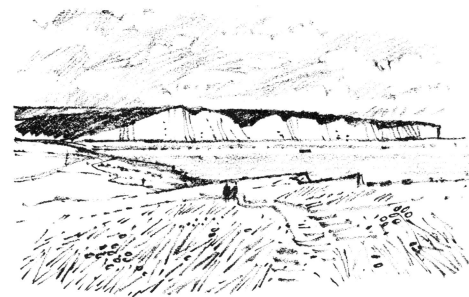

Carbon pencil on illustration board

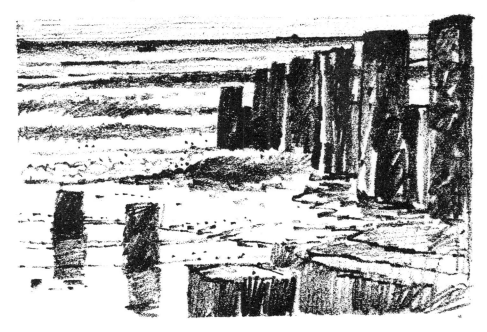

Carbon pencil on smooth
cartridge paper

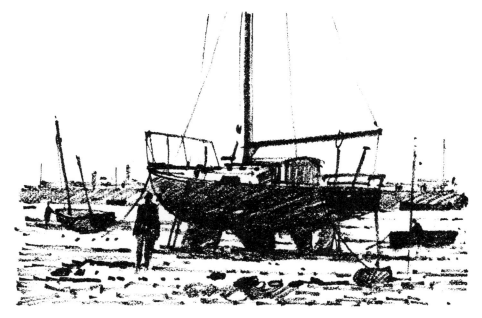

Carbon pencil on pastel paper

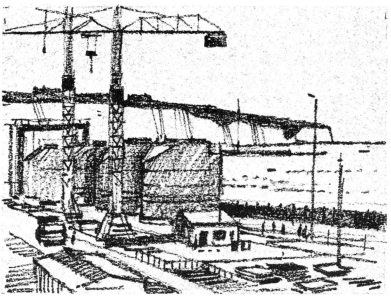

Carbon pencil on watercolour
paper

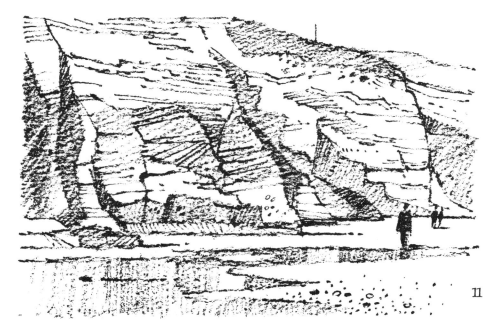

Where to draw

The contrasting subjects on this page illustrate only two examples of places you might choose to draw; there are plenty of others in the book. In the first of these, I started by positioning the tall buildings of the power station, since they are a principal part of the composition. Diminishing verticals such as breakwater posts and figures create distance and break up the essentially horizontal picture.

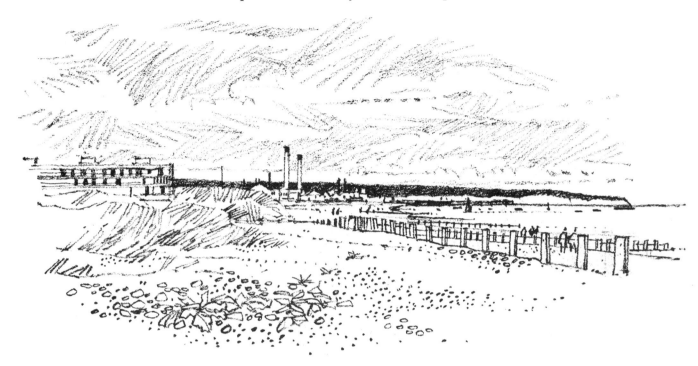

The tin mine shaft in the second drawing is perched several hundred feet above sea-level. I made a point of including the beach because the dimunitive figures and boat give scale and distance. Notice that variations in texture are suggested by only a few lightly-sketched details of stone and brick.

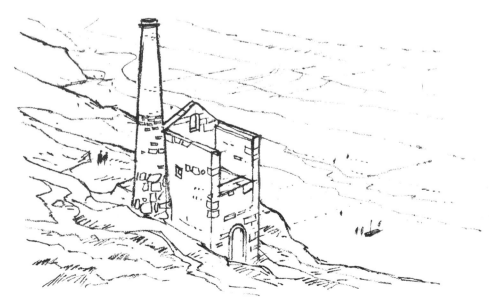

Perspective

Getting your drawing to look right is more important than striving for extreme accuracy of perspective. But if you follow a few very simple rules, perspective should not present problems. This pencil drawing of a promenade and the diagram below illustrate some of them:

Parallel lines above eye-level go down, and those above go up, to meet at the same vanishing point. Look at the poles and paving stones.

Objects diminish in size towards the horizon. Look at the figures and breakwater.

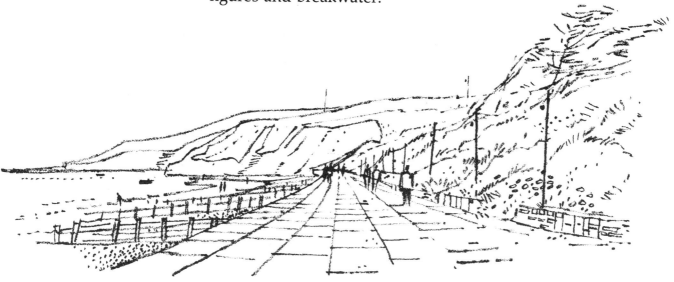

If you can see the side of something, two vanishing points are necessary. (To determine your eye-level, hold a pencil lengthways and horizontal at arm's length in line with your eyes.)

The angle between uprights is constant. Diagonal lines on the right of the diagram show how this helps to place equi-distant verticals.

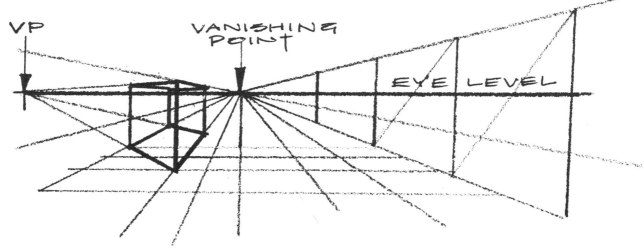

Composition

The top drawing illustrates a number of common mistakes in composition, which the bottom drawing corrects.

The large cloud is too near the middle, too pronounced, and running off the edge.

The distant cliff, middle distance and mast are also too central.

The middle land strip curves up too strongly.

The figures are too far to the side.

The foreground boat is too prominent.

The foreground fringe of stones (in a landscape it is often grass) is a pity.

The distant boat (left) should either be out of the picture or brought into it.

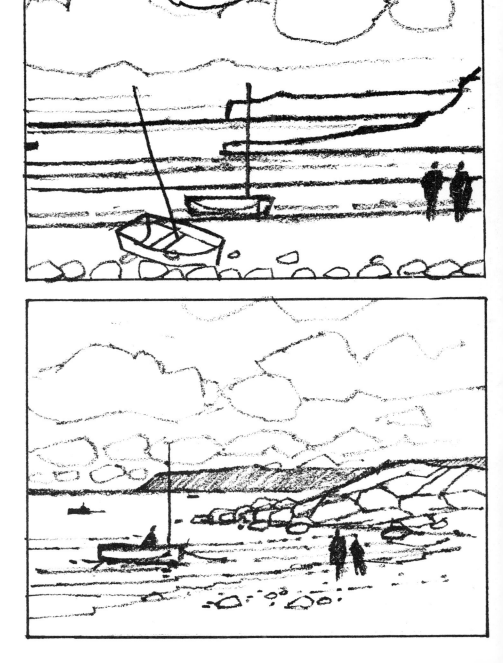

Where to begin a drawing

For a subject whose main features depend on the placing of horizontals, start by establishing the most important horizontal.

In stage two I sketched-in the areas of main interest—the cliff and houses. Then I shaded in the cliff as a background.
In stage three I added more shading to the houses and the sea, to lend contrast between the main areas of light and dark.

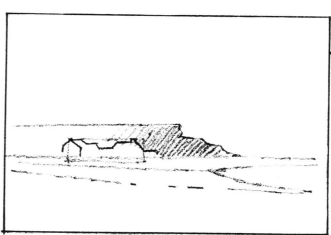

Finally, I added detail, in the form of a boat and figures, to suggest distance and scale. The detail in the foreground creates a feeling of recession in the drawing.

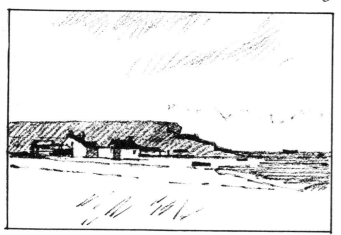
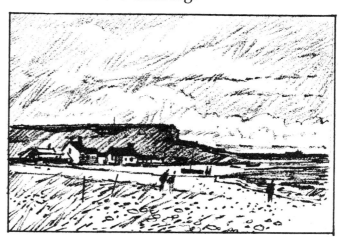

Again—in both these carbon pencil sketches of clouds and sea—I started by establishing the main horizontal—the horizon. The dark headland and sea came next, and then I built up more tones in the sky. Notice how the pencil lines have been left open to lend vigour to the drawing.

When putting tone into a drawing, start with strong light and dark only; then build up intermediate tones, leaving out those which are indecisive. This will give your drawing strength.

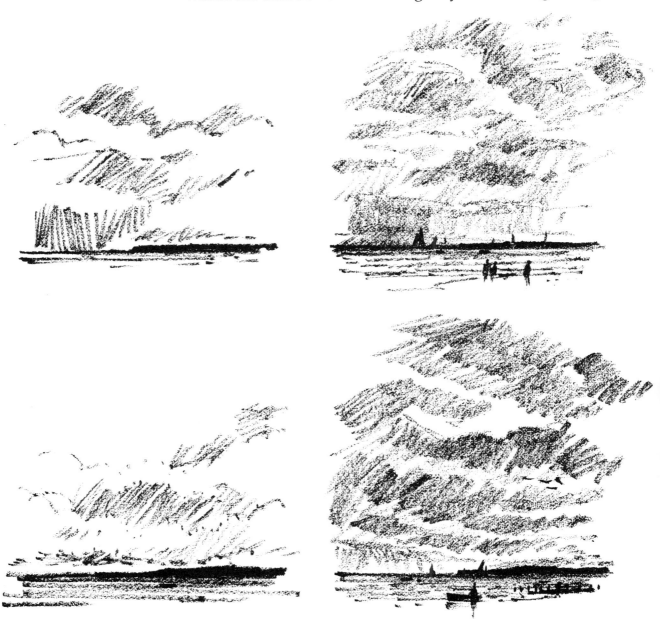

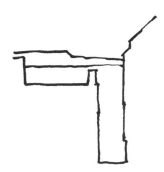

The most important part of this view is the distant sea between the buildings. I was careful to place it well off-centre and not to make it too pronounced.

The sketch on the left shows how I started my drawing.

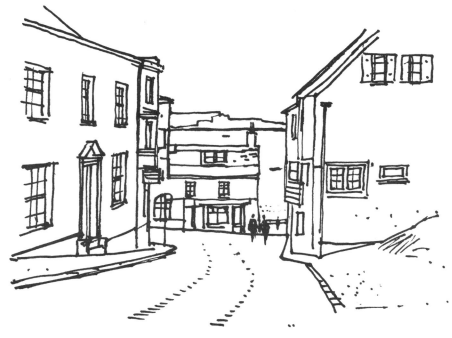

Here, several points of interest competed for attention—the clock tower, the horizontal line of the pier, and the acute angle of the promenade. I began by positioning the clock tower.

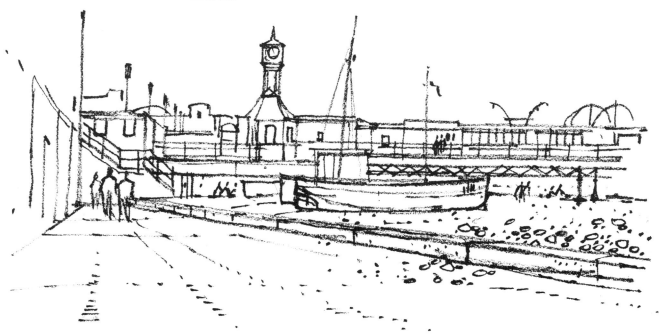

17

Waves: formation and movement

In order to study the movement and formation of a wave, I took some 35mm black and white photographs. I wanted, not to copy the photographs, but to make my own interpretation of the knowledge they gave me. These three drawings illustrate the development I learned.

In the first, the wave gathers up to form a broken crest. The back is higher than the front and begins to move forward. You can just see the dark patch on top. A strong wind whips the spray as the wave takes shape.

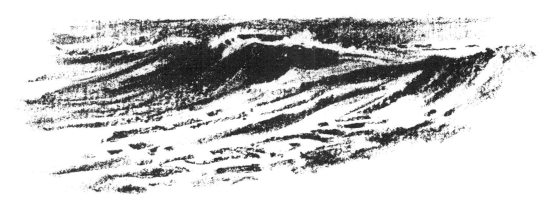

In the second drawing, that dark patch on the crest has swept forward into a curved wall of water. The action is a pronounced fall over an opposing upward sweep. A ridge is already extending along the wave as it rolls forward.

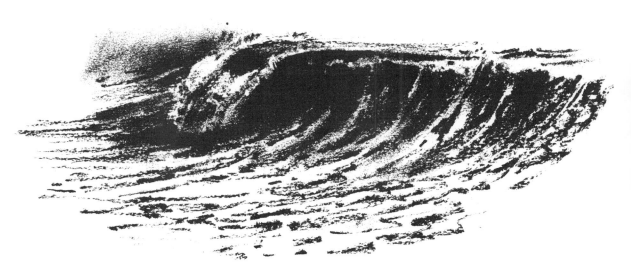

In the third drawing, the first part of the wave has broken and dispersed in a cloud of spray. The top part leaps forward with a continuous movement of curling, falling, and gathering up, until the wave loses momentum.

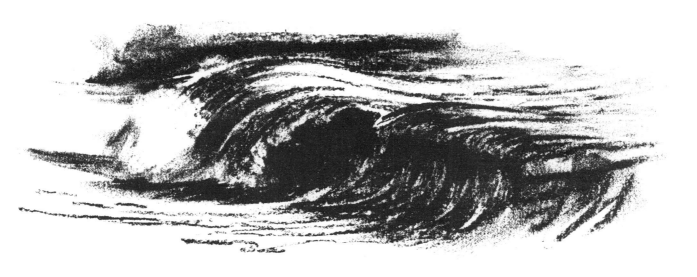

This final study in charcoal was done on the spot; I tried to capture the wave as it began to break.

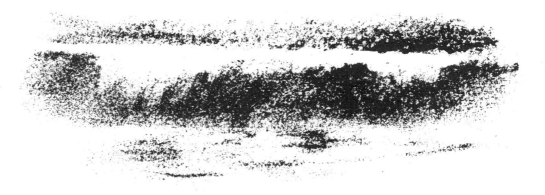

Waves: perspective

Perspective gives the impression of distance. Waves appear closer together as they recede toward the horizon. These lines may be parallel or diagonal to the horizon, depending on the direction of the tide.

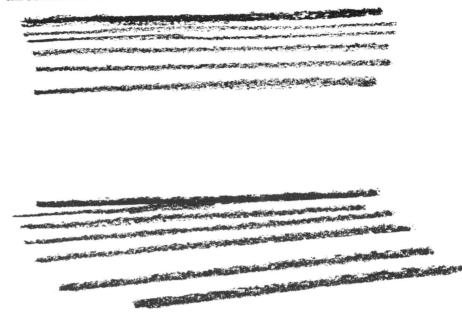

As well as appearing closer together the further away they are, waves become less distinct in shape. Near the horizon, lines may not be visible at all.

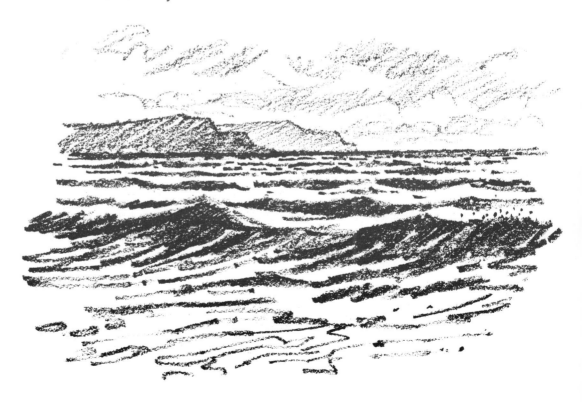

The rock and pebbles in this charcoal sketch suggest distance between the foreground and the waves. The pebbles also indicate scale.

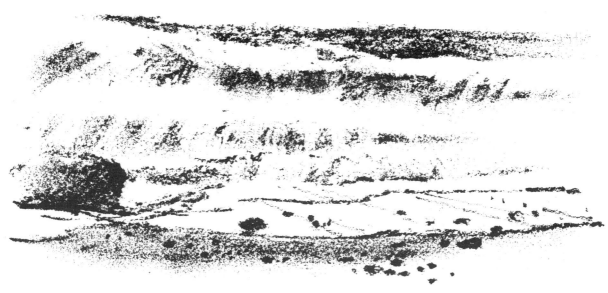

Figures in the second (charcoal and carbon pencil) sketch here also give scale and distance. Lighter tones toward the horizon help the picture to recede and aid aerial perspective.

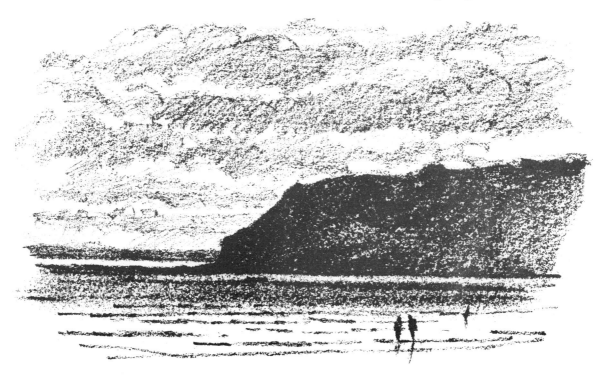

Waves:
step-by-step

I started this charcoal sketch by establishing the two largest rocks. Then I studied the movement of the water before attempting to draw the final picture.

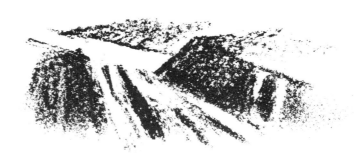

Concentrating my attention on just a small area of sea and rocks, I took twenty minutes to complete the sketch. The greater part of that time was spent in observation.

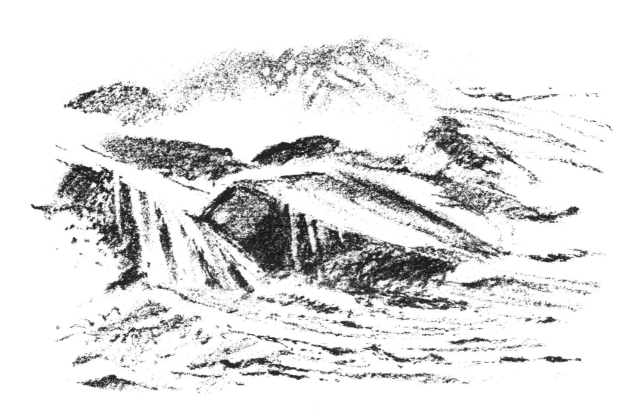

Beach scenes

This coastline sketch in carbon pencil concentrates on the rhythmic line of the cliffs, with only a suggestion of texture.

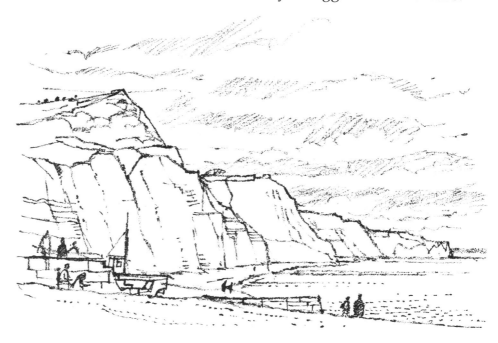

The second drawing is a tonal sketch in charcoal, showing the cliff mass. If you cover up the foreground figures, you will see how important they are in giving scale.

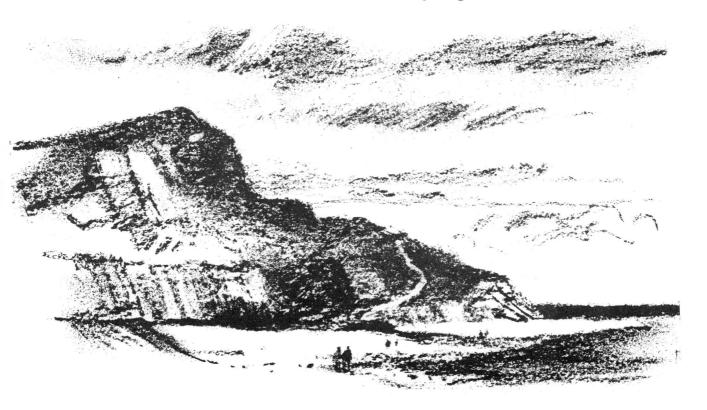

It is easy in a subject like this to make the cliff too dark and therefore overpowering. I deliberately made it much lighter than it was—lightly rubbing in some charcoal and then lifting out the lighter areas. Dark accents came last. Once again, cover up the tiny figures and notice that scale and distance is lost.

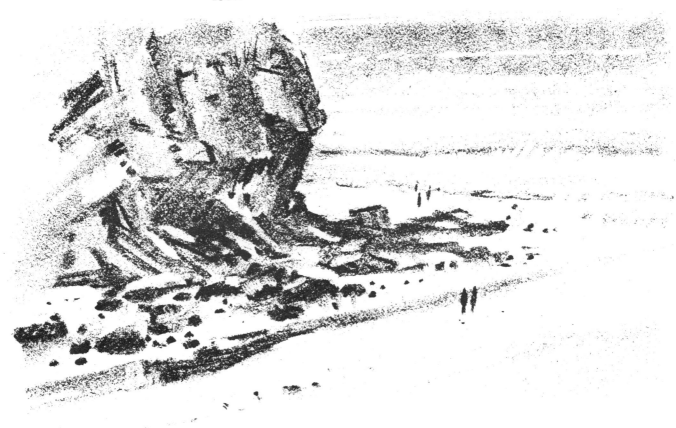

Oil pastel is a coarse medium but capable of versatility in line and tone. This outdoor sketch is a simple statement of an interesting view.

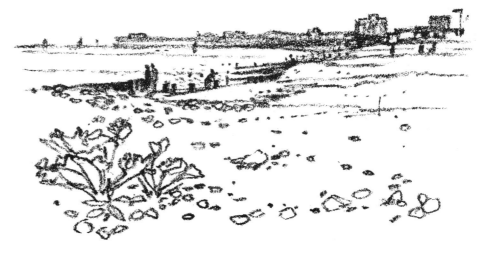

Bait diggers on wet sand are the subject of the charcoal drawing below. As usual, I started by indicating the horizon line. Then I lightly rubbed in some charcoal over sky and sea, adding a few extra darks in places. Next I put in the figures and added detail to the foreground.

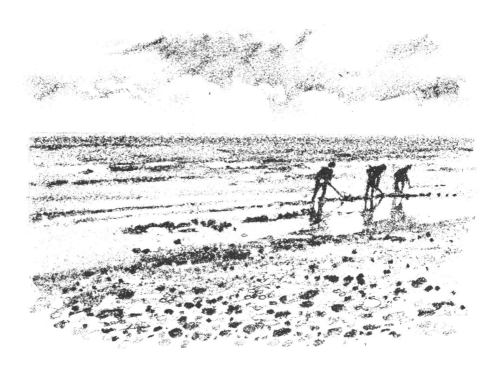

Oil pastel is ideal for broad simple statements such as this. I was interested in the similarity of hut roofs and church spire.

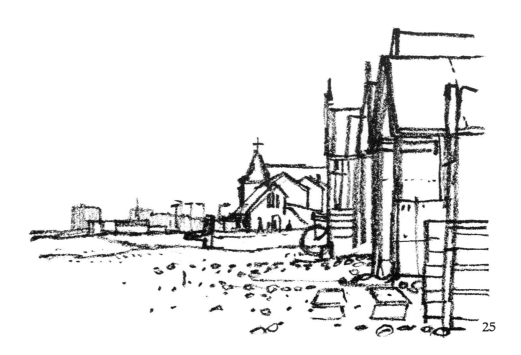

I made this charcoal drawing from a black-and-white photograph—not copying, but trying to catch the mood of the scene itself. The result is a simple statement. I avoided detail on the breakwater, which would distract attention from the breaking wave caught in the wind.

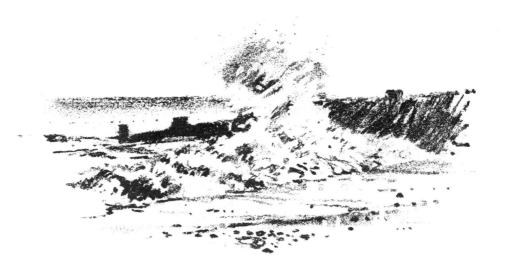

I like the naturalness of the composition in crayon, but there is a small fault. The upright of the metal stand should cut across the bow of the boat, rather than lying right against it.

Sitting down to draw can often produce a more interesting viewpoint than standing up, and it is easier to keep your equipment stable.

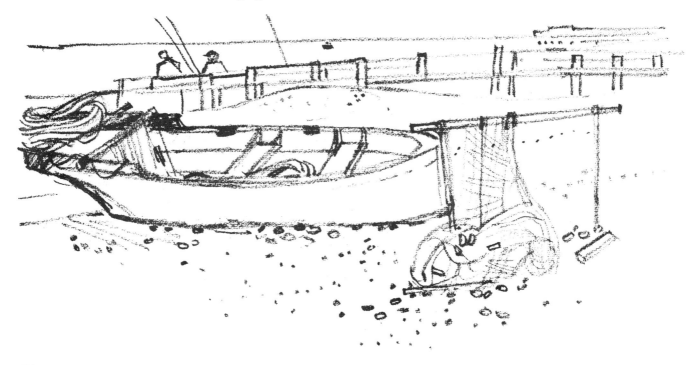

The top, carbon-pencil drawing shows the value of a dark area in the background. It adds interest to the picture, and links the far distance with the cliffs. Notice the difference if you cover up the dark background line.

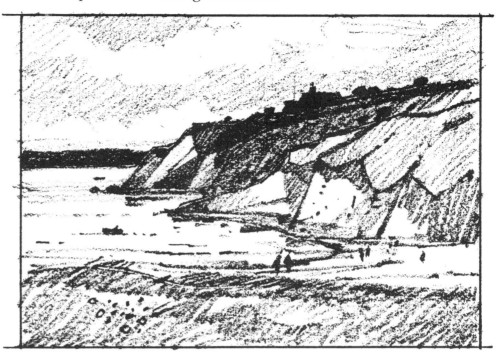

The sketch below was made partly with a broad chunky marker pen and partly with the fine line of a ball point. Where the rigging ran across dark areas I took it out with a sharp knife.

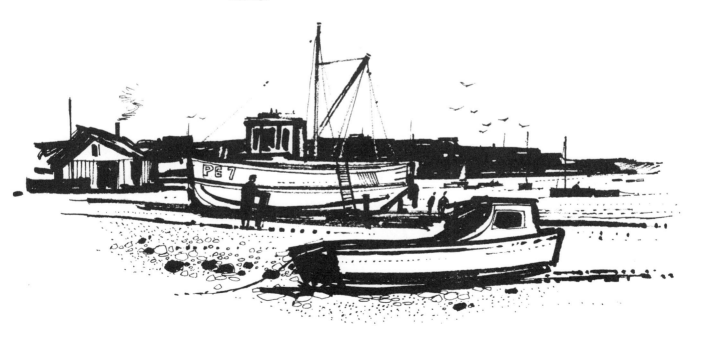

Drawing parts

This is a drawing of a small section of seascape. Its main interest is in the undulating geological strata and great clefts in the cliffs. Indicating scale is very important. The figures here suggest the grandeur of the cliff, even though only part of the rock face is shown. The ebbing tide left pools on the beach, and I have carried cliff reflections into them, linking beach and cliff together.

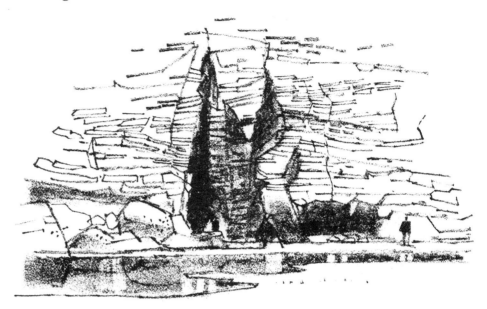

Stones, shells and seaweed are part of a beach's 'furniture'. Try drawing them with the aid of a powerful magnifying glass to bring out their texture and pattern. The drawings here (of a worn shell, and a piece of seaweed clasping a pebble) are much bigger than the objects themselves.

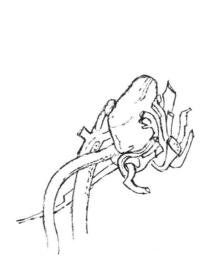

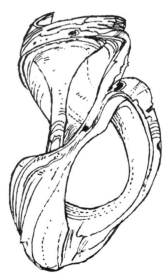

The pencil drawing here—of a breakwater and the pebbles
wedged between its weathered timbers—makes an interesting
composition. The high horizon emphasises the slope of the
breakwater and provides an opportunity to add background
detail.

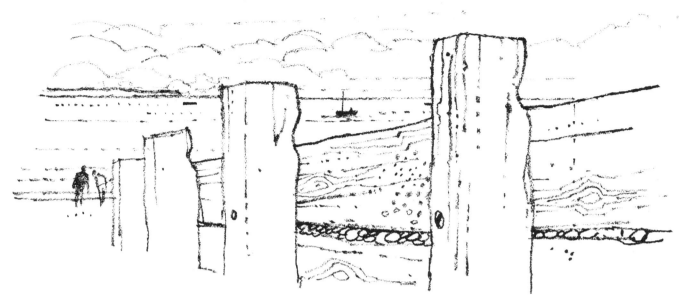

The ball-point sketches show enlarged details of an old lobster
pot. Rusted wire still holds the iron rods firmly and makes
interesting patterns. Drawing a complete lobster pot is
difficult. Try drawing parts of it first. Don't do any shading;
go for texture by descriptive line.

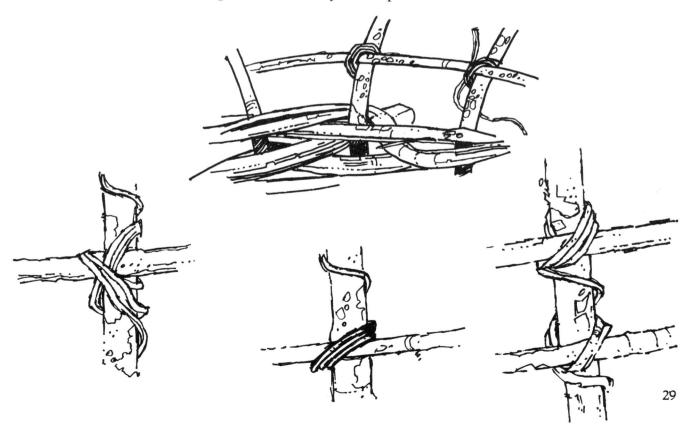

Sketches

Sketching can produce drawings that are complete in themselves or ideas and visual notes for a fuller picture later, or it can be simply fun. The next few pages show a variety of examples.

Don't always go for full tonal drawings. This crayon line-drawing picks out patterns of shape and contrasts of texture without using tone. Notice the contrast between the solid cottages, sitting square and firm, and the tree bent in growth by sea winds; and (in the foreground) stones of a dry wall and thin, spiky grasses.

The sketch below of a container vessel was made with a carbon pencil. I prevented the wooden marker buoy being too dominant by joining it up to the ship.

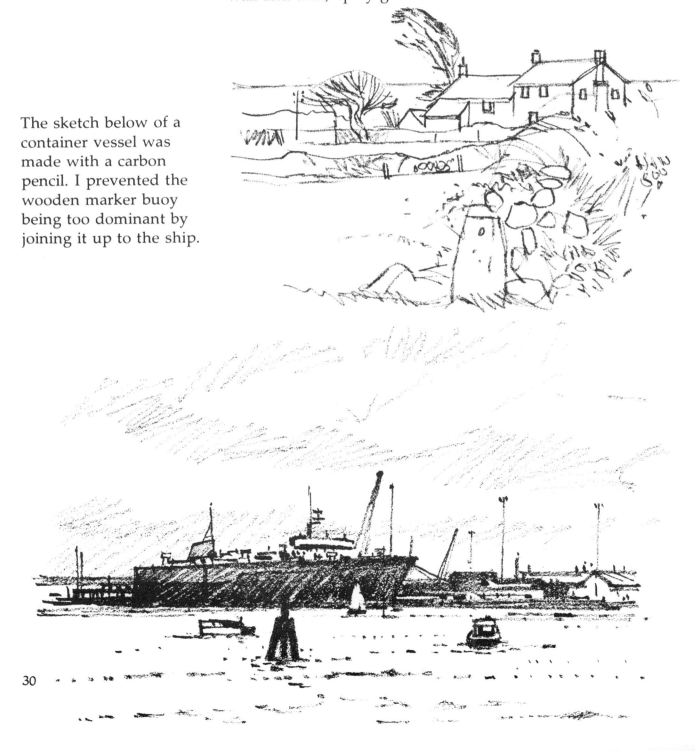

I drew this charcoal sketch with my back toward the direction of the sea. An estuary contains many objects of interest to an artist: fishing boats on mud flats, flimsy-looking gangplanks, tarred sheds, winching tackle. There are enough subjects just off the sea to fill many sketchbooks.

When drawing with charcoal outdoors, fix the result immediately with charcoal fixative to prevent smudging. You can always draw on top of the fixative when it is dry, and then fix again.

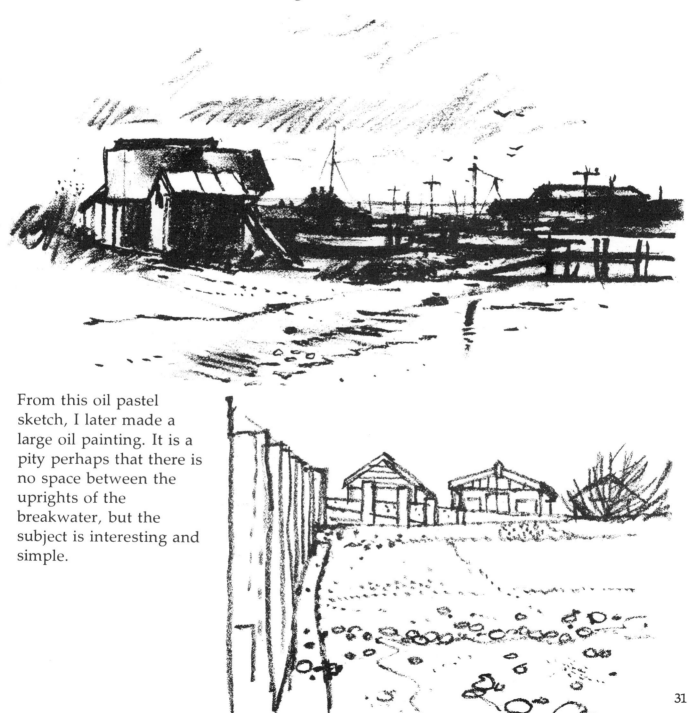

From this oil pastel sketch, I later made a large oil painting. It is a pity perhaps that there is no space between the uprights of the breakwater, but the subject is interesting and simple.

Small preliminary carbon sketches like these can solve problems which would waste a lot of time if you left them till you started on a large drawing. If one of them doesn't work, make another rectangle (the originals of these measured no more than 2″ × 1½″) and start again. Never try to make a pretty sketch. An honest drawing has much more value.

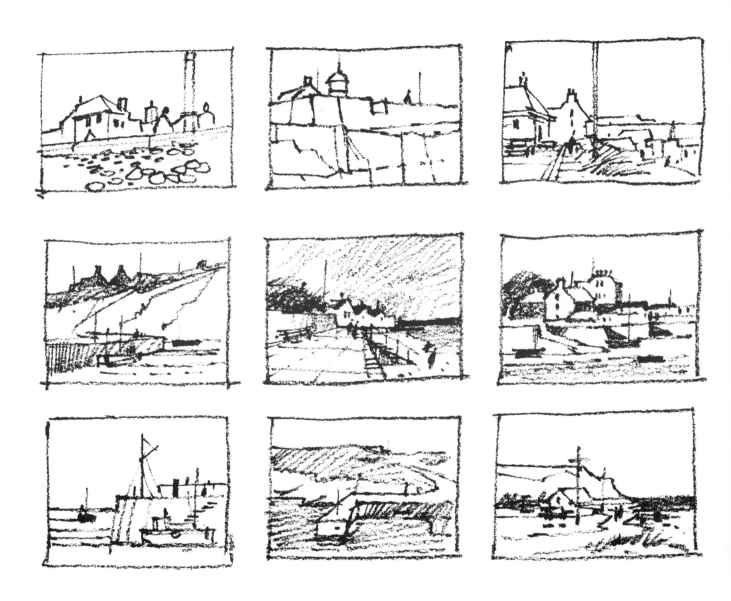

Bad weather need not deter you from drawing. I made this charcoal sketch, with a cup of tea near me, in the warmth and comfort of a hotel. The sea was a yellow brown and the sky a steely grey. I drew the pier first, and then the rolling waves pounding in to the shore. The sea was dark, but to give the picture tonal balance I made the pattern of the pier darker still.

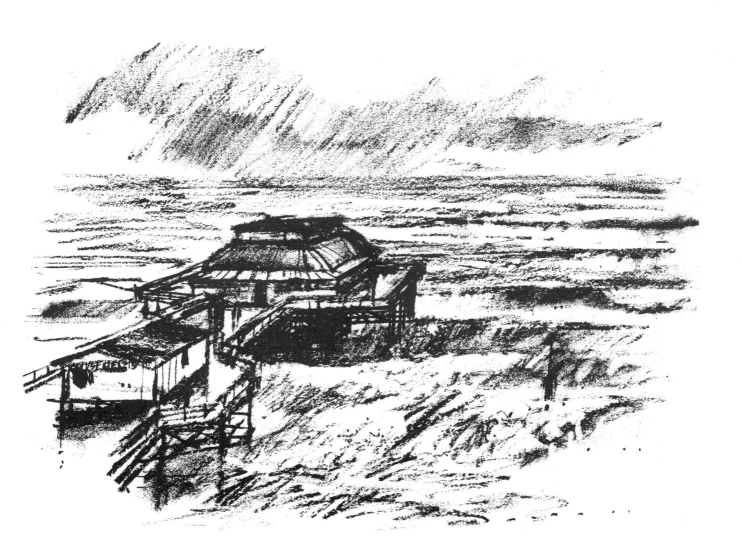

Blocking and shading

Notice that the pencil drawing here of cliff tops has three basic tones, and the pen sketch of the clock tower only two.

When making a tonal drawing, begin by blocking-in with line, and then proceed with shading. It is simpler to start shading with only two degrees of light and dark. Then, as the drawing progresses half-tones can be added with discretion. Remember to keep lines open and let the paper show through.

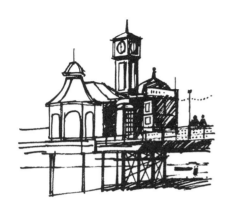

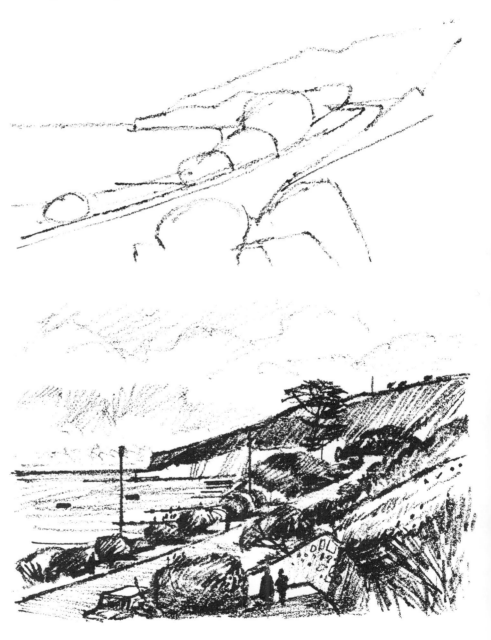

These two tonal drawings illustrate different charcoal techniques. In the top one, I lightly rubbed the charcoal over the paper, and then lifted out the light areas with a putty eraser. (If charcoal is rubbed in too heavily, it gets into the fibres of the paper and highlights cannot be restored.) In places, I used my fingers to 'blend' the drawing. The cliff silhouette helps to create the effect of back lighting, and its flatness contrasts with the textured sky.

The bottom drawing was made without blending or lifting out; it is a direct charcoal sketch. Maximum boldness was achieved by keeping shading to simple statements.

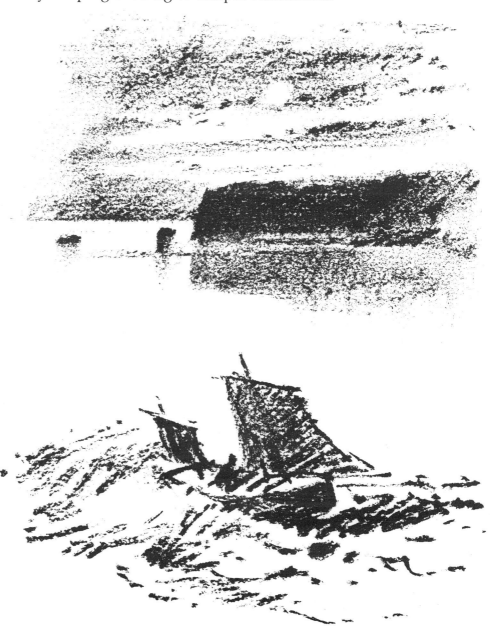

Getting life into a drawing

The top four scribbles on this page were made with a carbon pencil, the lower two with an HB. They show that too much rubbing makes for smudgy dullness; a drawing can have more life if the marks are open. In the lower drawing you can see how this works.

Practice short pencil scribbles like those above. Then do a **simple drawing** with three or four tones of shading.

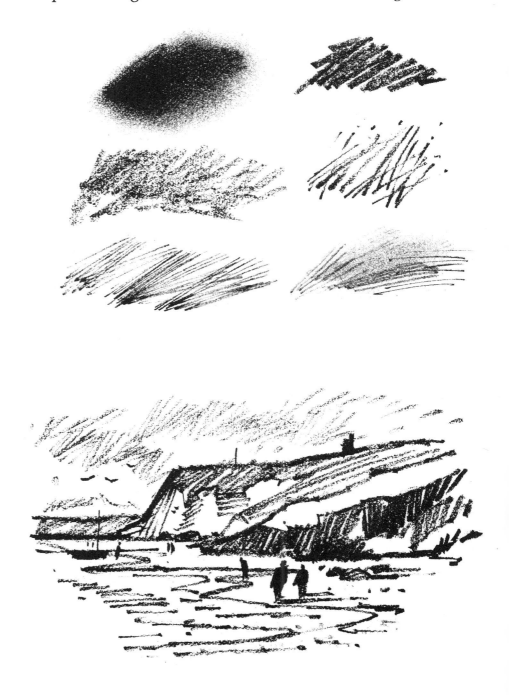

Horizontal lines convey repose. By simply placing an opposing vertical, you can give life to the composition—as in the drawing here. Obviously this is an extreme statement—not always desirable or practical, depending on the subject—but it's worth knowing. Figures, used similarly, can be more subtle and add more life.

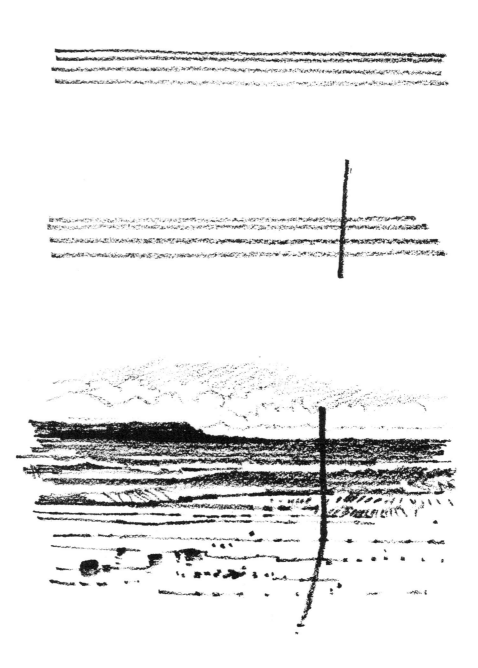

Correcting mistakes

In the top carbon-pencil drawing the features are badly placed, and the picture is spoiled by the bottom fringe of grasses. (Compare the drawing below.) Mistakes like these are difficult to correct; they are best avoided by making exploratory sketches first which contain the main shapes and patterns—such as the roughs shown here.

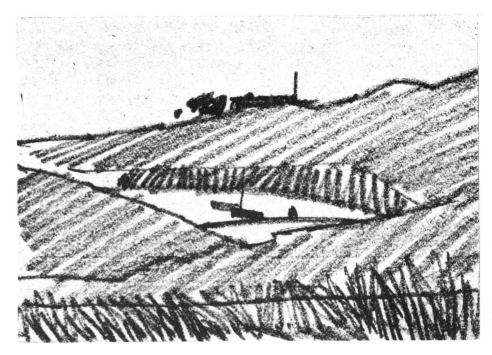

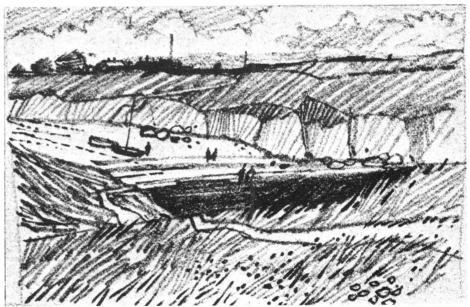

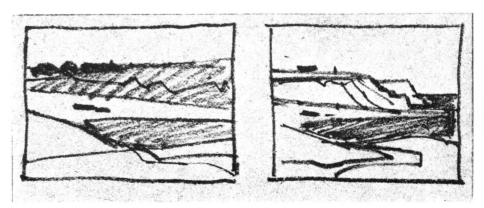

It is easier to correct mistakes in charcoal and pastel, which are dry and soft, than in other mediums. The preliminary blocking-in of the top drawing was made with a carbon pencil. It would be difficult to remove the lines without spoiling the paper surface; not so the charcoal shading.

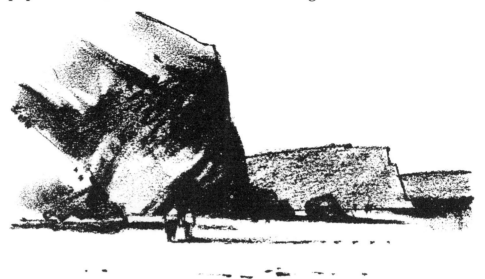

The 'mistake' I made in the lower drawing was to begin with the wrong medium. I wanted to use a felt tip pen, but changed my mind because the weather changed—for the worse. I drew over the pen drawing with wax crayon and then on top of that again with the pen. It is often better to start a drawing outdoors with a broad medium.

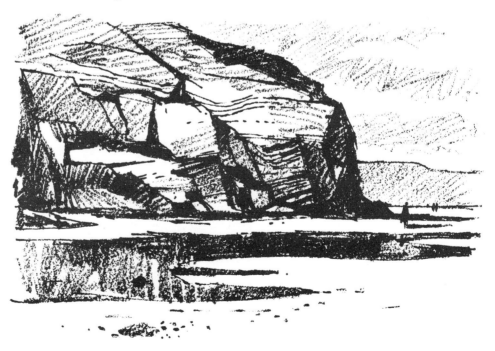

Common problems

One of the commonest problems is getting the right contrast between light and dark. Correct tone values are important in a drawing that contains shading. The sketches here show how to achieve contrast and dimension by dividing the picture into separate planes, each with a different tone. The smaller sketch has three tones—dark, medium, and light; if you are a beginner, it is worth trying early on a similar tone drawing to this very simple beach scene.

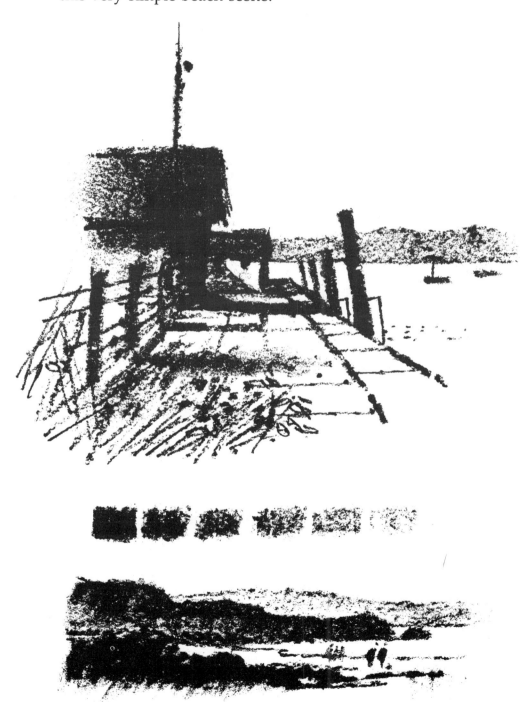

Knowing when to stop is another common problem. Here, it was very tempting to add more tone and detail to the sea. The result would have been a loss of spontaneity and freshness. When you think you are half-finished, pause to consider whether there is in fact anything more to do. You may be surprised to find your drawing looks complete.

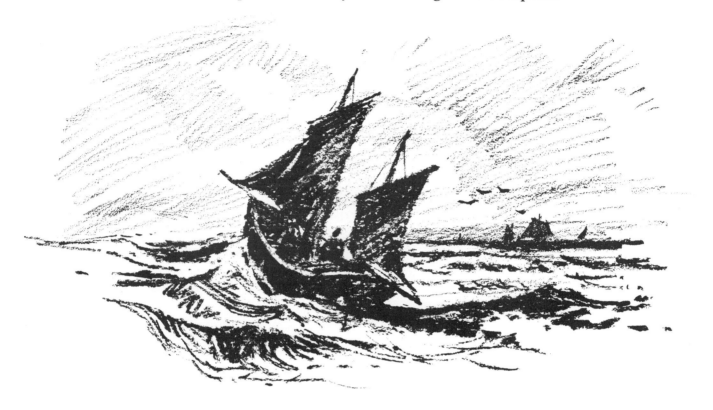

Different subjects/ different techniques

The top sketch here was made with charcoal and soft, white Conté on medium-grey pastel paper. The greyness gives the picture an extra tone, and the grain of the paper—where it is left visible—provides a sparkling texture. Conté over charcoal becomes muddy, so the light areas had to be kept free of charcoal.

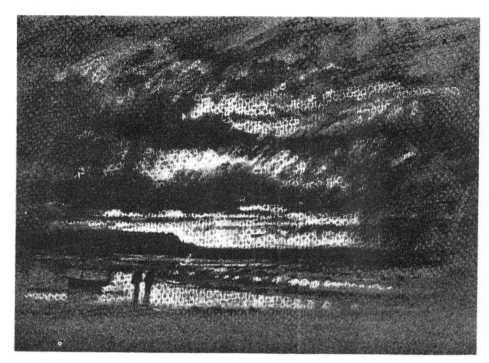

Below: Raw sienna pastel was loosely applied to cartridge paper and, without fixing, I drew with a black ball-point pen on top. You can achieve similar background effects with acrylic or watercolour. I put the seaweed under a magnifying glass and have drawn it larger than life size.

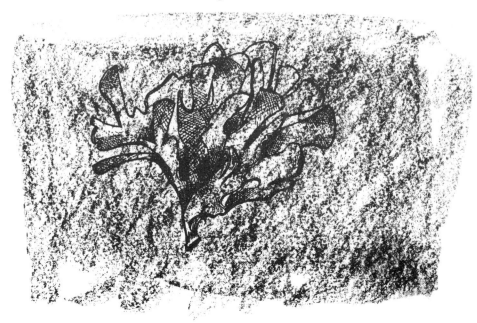

The first drawing here was made with a carbon pencil—which does not allow erasing and therefore encourages freshness. Unlike ordinary pencil, a carbon line does not shine. My sketch is deliberately loose in order to show the pencil strokes to advantage.

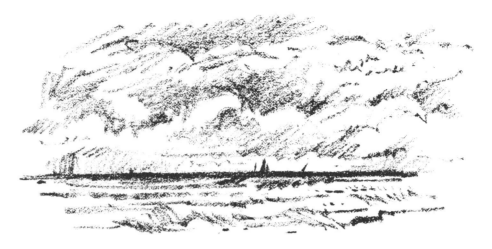

The charcoal drawing below is based on an oil painting. I started by lightly rubbing in charcoal with a paper tissue, then drew on to this surface with willow charcoal. As the drawing progressed, I lifted out light areas with a putty eraser. The main point of the wave impact in the background gives depth to the picture and a focal point. Notice, too, how the foreground splash tapers in toward the background.

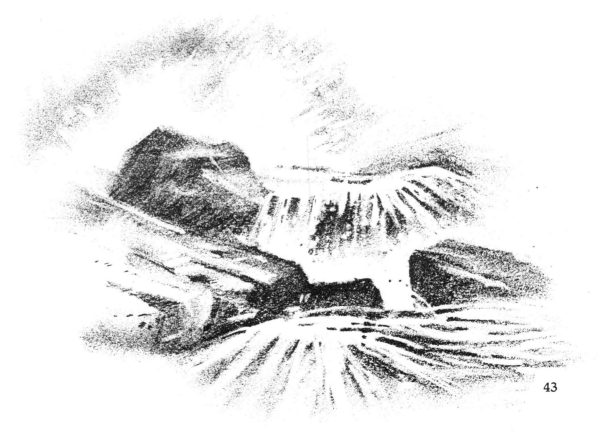

In the first of the four stages shown here, the charcoal was lightly drawn over the paper (if you press too hard, you will leave a dark mark). In the second, I rubbed over the charcoal with my fingers, again lightly, to even out the tone, but the result was too dark to show up my drawing, so I gently rubbed the surface with a tissue.

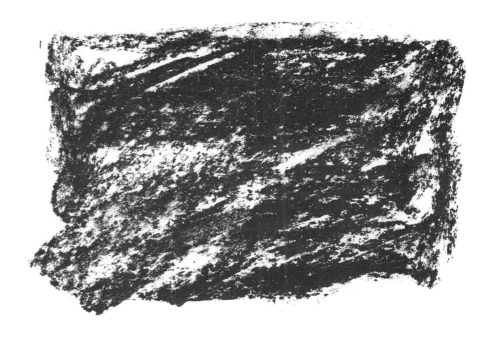

In the third stage, I positioned the main part of the subject. In the final drawing, light areas were lifted out with a kneaded putty eraser. For fine detail I used a carbon pencil, although charcoal pencil would have done just as well.

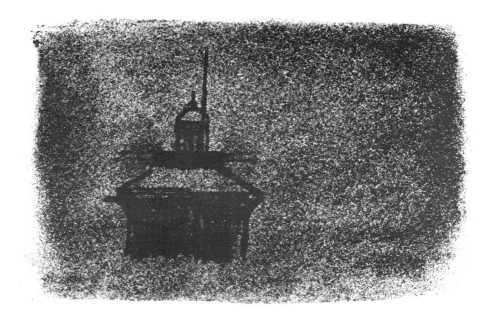

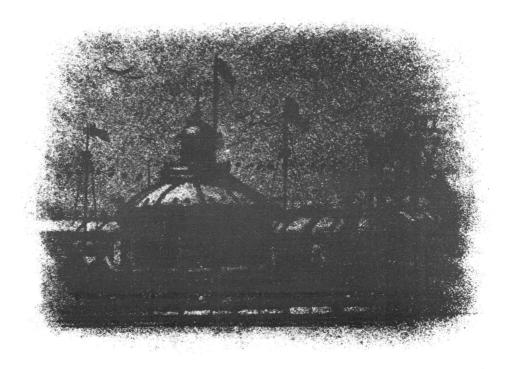

Brush-drawing is a strong, expressive technique, much practised in China and Japan, but less so in the Western World. Experience is necessary to produce successful results.

Choice of paper texture determines the quality of brush marks. In the first drawing here, I used watercolour paper, and drew directly onto it (no preliminary pencil sketch) with a sable brush and black writing ink.

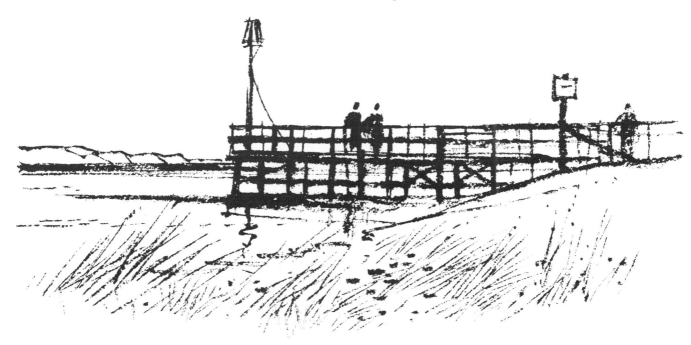

The second sketch is a combination of charcoal and brush drawing. I rubbed in the charcoal to get an even tone, and then drew directly on top with a brush. Afterwards, I lifted out the light areas from the charcoal with a putty eraser.

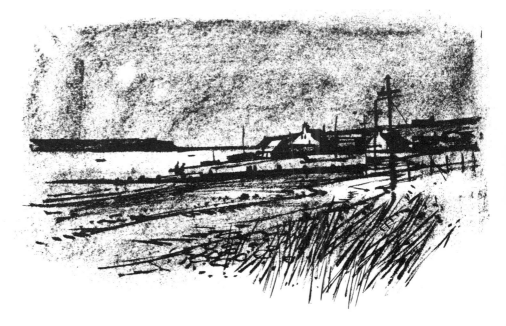

The top sketch here was made with a 6B pencil on watercolour paper. Soft pencils can produce a wide range of tone values and can be used in combination with other grades.

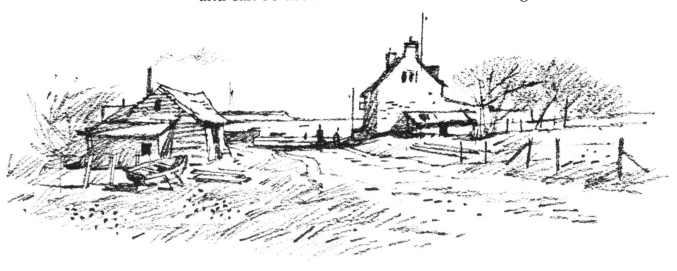

The sketch below was made with a black felt-tip pen on watercolour paper, which breaks up the pen line. Notice that there is not much shading here. I kept to line in order to emphasize shapes.

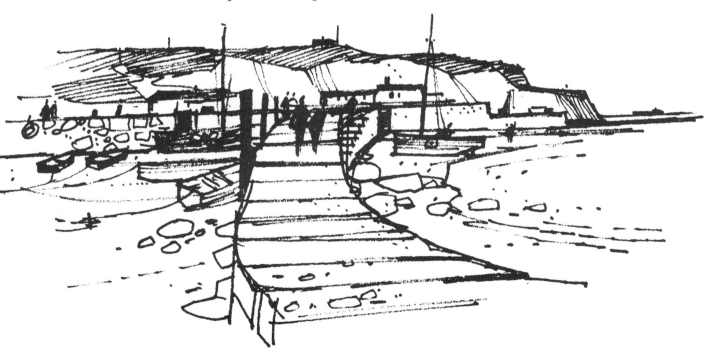

Charcoal is an excellent medium for small or large drawings, and still underrated. The top drawing here was made with willow charcoal, using the charcoal-tone background technique. I put no charcoal where the sun's orb is, to allow the whiteness of the paper to shine through.

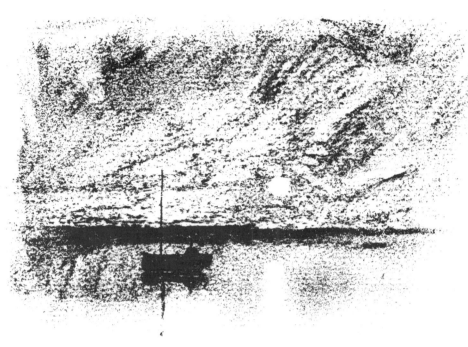

The chisel-shaped lead of a soft carpenter's pencil makes a mark of its own. In the lower drawing here, I used it on watercolour paper and deliberately kept the marks open so that they could be seen easily. You can make a needle-thin line or a broad stroke with this pencil.

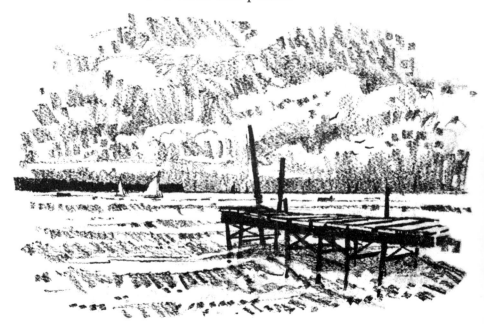